Moonlit Verses

Maari raja

To you, Paris

I dedicate this to you,
sweet friend.

I will cherish you forever,
until this life ends.

May your smile spread
far and wide,

curing those who could
never find a way to mend.

May your purity live on

And Let the Moon Shine

Ignorant Affections

I never knew what love was
until I started
smiling in your absence,
You became the reason to live
and why I
forgot the sorrow that I had then.

Sinful Living

You truly loved
to live and sin,
enjoying life's caress
upon your skin.
You did not act with
a second to think
because in the race of life,
you only wanted to win.

A Map of Stars

the sun and moon are this world's lamps,
lights that guide us through the night.
The stars are like specks laid out as a map,
perhaps to lead me to you and you to I.
I will not question the love we once had,
but I will ask, where are you tonight?
Memories will always stay in the past,
yet I will always think of when you were mine.

Echo's Memory

Her name carved into memory
as an echo.
A boundless voice of thought
that will never set me free
or let go.

Leftover Memories

I once dared not love,
oaths I had taken.
it had all changed
when I felt your touch,
that dark night
when it was raining.
Images of us,
of you and I
are the only
memories remaining.

Whilst you love another

I've watched you love
another lucky soul,
and it's what hurts the most.
I still think of what could have been,
Me and you, you and me, us,
just a wish that haunts my dream
even after I've grown old.

Inception

I still crave your love and affection,
the desire to kiss you was the inception.
But life kept me away from you
and so I suffered depression.
My thoughts always mention,
in a conversation to myself,
the mistakes I made with no correction,
and even when I tried,
It was too late.
You're happier now
with no regrets and past reflections.

A Moonlit View

Have you ever dreamed about
a life lived under the moonlight?
The painted black skies of night,
stars embedded like jewels
on a canvas so beautifully profound.
The galaxies like a cosmic pool,
with planets like marbles alight,
and a silence in the darkness,
a beauty without sound.
A wonder no poetic serenade
could ever truly define,
no word, no sentence,
no song of rhyme.

Our Song

It's been 4 summers long,
I still hear the lyrics of our songs.
The words are still clear,
they do not fade
no matter how much time has gone.
The whispers of my love,
can you still hear
how much I chant your name?

Forgotten Promise

my soul is torn,
my heart is broken.

What is this storm
in this darkened moment?
a conflict of whispers,
thoughts in my mind.

Their echoes linger
to destroy my life.
this cold of solitude,
memories of past.

I remember our promise too,
but that never stayed intact.

I have loved you since,
and I'll love you forever.

I love you now, my bliss,
even if we will never be together.

Through Darkness & Light

Though the twilight hour
may cover us in dark.
remember the highlighted flowers
that heal our hearts.

The sun may set into night
but it shall certainly rise again.
There is no end to our light
so let us continue on our pens.

Some Men & Love

Men are often too blinded by pride
to understand the tears
in a woman's eyes.
Men are often too deaf from life,
to be able to hear the pleas
that a woman has cried.
Men are often too dumb from love
to comprehend the pain
that the women will fight.
**Some men just do not love
the way a woman does.**

Educational Kiss

I was ignorant of love,
until I was
educated by your touch.
Your kiss taught me
everything I needed to
know about us.

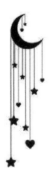

Cupid's Arrow

Never mind,
I will love your shadow
until I am deserving of you.
Desperate for your love,
hit by his arrow,
No one can love you like I do.

At First Sight

All my life,
I had only dreamt.
Of falling in love.
Of feeing that touch.
I never understood
what it meant,
until I met you
and fell in love
at first sight.

The Love of a Woman

A woman's tears
doesn't mean she's weak.
It doesn't mean
she's projecting her fears
or failure of her dreams.

It means she loved truly,
far beyond what you deserve.
This is an incomprehensible beauty,
may women always be preserved.

The World is Encompassed

The painted skies of blue
really seem like a dream.
Are they really just
a reflection of the sea?
If this world is
encompassed by such,
then what have
we really seen?

Travelling Thoughts

Have you ever pondered upon
that which is beyond thought?
beyond imagination that is gone,
things that have never been seen before.

has your mind ever travelled,
to a realm that succeeds dreams?
A dimension that contains no planets,
or any mysteries that can be seen.

If this world is but a marble
on the canvas of the universe,
then the skies aren't really a marvel,
because there is something
far beyond this earth.

Often

We often pursue our desires
and the pleas of our wishes.
We often extinguish the fires
that push for our souls
to be spiritually lifted.
We often ignore our
hearts when they retire,
and look for another journey
to the place where bliss is.

Too Soon

My life began when
I fell in love with you.

And It had ended when
life had ended us too soon.

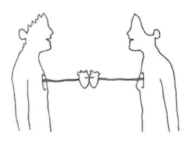

Still Seeking You

I still see your face,
somewhere in the clouds.

I still hear your name,
like thunder,
an echoing sound.

My heart is still in pain,
from when I had lost you
to never again be found.

Now you rest in the heavens,
amongst the other angels.

You travel through paradise
as another blessing
with my love that you cradle.

Are you looking down at me,
my love?

Cause I'm still looking for you
even though I'm here
and you're far above.

Can't Stop Loving You

I don't have the strength

to stop

loving you.

Let me find my death,

yet I'll still

continue

loving you

A Sacred Life

Sacred are the winds of life
that caress our skins so gently.

They embrace us with great ambience,
life's magic flows in our veins intensely.
Sapphire blue that stretches across the
skies,

like a beautiful painting on a canvas so white.
The morning sun illuminating the lands,
from horizon to horizon,
far beyond the reach of our eyes.

The winds that whisper secrets,
unheard from our ears yet revealed.
They are in front of us,
as we behold and yield
to this universe's sequence.

Love Story

My mind will die.
My soul will die.
My heart will die.
Yet the remnants of your love,
the memories of us,
they shall remain
as our legacy.
A love story none
can ever defy.

A Prayer to The Stars

what is left of my heart
but a piece that still loves?
the rest scattered with the winds,
like ashes, somewhere far,
my love was never enough.
My soul has fallen into dark,
being tortured by my sins
and the memories of us.
I wonder still
If my prayers
ever reach the stars.

Love's Essence

When all words
seem to be lost,
when poems no
longer flow.
When songs now
sound wrong,
when stories
become old.
The essence of love
has left this world.

To the Love

I dedicated this to Shakespeare
who knew love with his words.

I dedicate this to Romeo
who knew love with his death.

Stories that travelled this world
And became examples to no end.

I dedicate this to the love
that became the names
upon our breath.

To the love that,
changed the relationship
between friends.

To the love that,
gave us hope to live again.
To the love that
caused beautiful dreams
in our heads.

This love is the love
that fuels the poet's ink.

Poems written that
shake the heavens above
and cause the clouds to sink.

Let us hope for a love
that becomes a legacy.

A love made from a single touch
and instilled into perfect memories.

A Permanent Stain

Here's to me hoping that
my tears will wash away the ink.

Whenever I begin to write again,
it's like a dart to my heart
and suddenly my soul begins to sink.

Your love still flows through my veins,
a poison that can't ever be extracted.

It hurts more upon mention of your name,
some new kind of plague in memories' flame,

and now my pen seems to be stuck and
stranded.

Why will the image of your face never leave,
it's a permanent stain on the walls of my
heart.

And every time I see it,
it becomes hard to breathe,
It's like I'm blinded again
and it's become so dark

Remember a time when I
used to smile and laugh,

now I still live, bereft of both
and walk while I bleed.

One Chance

Those words you had once spoken,
they still echo in my heart.
And although my heart is now broken,
I still hope for a light in the dark.

I still see your silhouette and shadow,
dancing to the rhythms of my heart beat.
Across those walls, so long and narrow,
whispers from above, as if the stars speak.

If I had once chance,
to reverse the sands of time.
I would redo the past,
and fight until

**you would always
be mine.**

Love After Death

I'm completely in love with you.
Always have been, always will
and even after I'm dead too.

My heart refuses to love another,
attraction exists, perhaps, for others
It will never be the same love,
the one I have for you,
from now until forever.

Moonlight Love

The moon and I used to speak,
we told each other secrets.

I told her about you and me,
and she was curious
about how we met.

And I told her,
It was under her light.

Under the sanctity
of her luminosity,
of a special night..

She was bright.

It was a fantasy.
Yet this was how
our love had started.

Under the moon light
that destroyed the darkness.
Our moon light love,
The story of our heart's bliss.

A Dark Betrayal

A dark betrayal.
I felt your action pierce my heart,
your falsehood was not veiled.
The truth has failed.
There's no light in the dark,
wherever disloyalty lies.
And although you may be pale,
your heart was blackened
once you stabbed me in the heart.

Forgive Me

and maybe I deserve recompense,
for all the mistakes I have made.
I've been making error ever since
my life commenced.

Forgive me, for I've an ill fate,
I find myself often in pain,
and it is often intense.
Forgive me.
I'm sorry
for extinguishing
the flames.

Thou Art Judas

Thou art Judas in but feminine form,
a rose with no petals, just prickly thorns.

You whisper and converse with the devils
wherein your shadows & silhouettes are born.

Veiled in a disguise considered
truth and level,
yet for those seeking the reality,
they shall see upon your head
those hellish horns.

You are a succubus born and bred,
filled with hatred and scorn.
Preying on innocent people
by pretending to be a "friend"
when in reality,
you are the devil's first born.

Burnt Love

my heart is but ashes,
grey dust of a burnt love.
Yet the pain is ever lasting
like the echoes that remember us,
because you were my first love.
I loved you from dawn till dusk,
something I did without you even asking.
I'm still haunted by memories of us,
not even your shadow is left to hug,
I'm living a dead life without your love.

Fade into Nothing

why is the feeling
of your touch lost to me?
why has the bleeding
of our love gone to sleep?

The pain kept me alive in
my reality and in my dreams,
now I just wish I'd fade
into the nothing we see.

why are the stars revealing
everything that's a lot to see,
that my destiny is concealing
everything I'm not to see,
And in all honesty?

I'll honestly,
never forget you my love.

Waltzing Hearts

It's a quiet morning,
I've just finished my shift.
My mind is wandering,
contemplating on the
things that I miss.
And with no surprise,
I see your face
and my heart starts
to break into bits.

Tears swelling up,
streaming down my face
like a cascading bliss.

Your shadow
fused with mine
as I still taste
the taste of your lips,
the taste of your kiss,
the moments I savoured
looking into your eyes.

Falling in love with you,
a blessing from the skies,
that today, painfully, I miss you.

Remember the romance
to which our hearts catered,
dancing to imagined melody,
waltzing to a steady tune.

Soul's Truth

Loving you is
all I knew.
In my mind,
it was you.
In my heart
it was you.
For my soul
you were truth.

Destined

maybe I'm destined
to fall in love
and never be able to stand up.
Never get to feel your touch,
or take your time,
will you ever step off
the pedestal that you stand on?

My heart is breaking again.

Bloodied Canvas

Rip my heart from my torso,
and the only thing you will find
in the stains of blood on the floor,
is your face etched into the crimson lines.

This is my love.
The only one in my heart.

Is this not enough
or must you find yourself
in an overwhelming dark?

How can I not know?

How can I not know love
when my heart beats only for thine melody?
How can I not yearn for "us"
when you have given me these memories?

How can I not long for your touch,
when even the blind can see this chemistry?
How can I not seek this love
when our story goes beyond Romeo's legacy?

The Answer in Your Smile

Sometimes
I question my heart.
I question myself.

I question the stars,
and if this is hell.

But then,
I see your smile...

And suddenly
everything has been answered.

Friendly Lover

I'm not the kinda guy you like,
not your usual type.
The fuck boys that break your heart,
I'm the one you talk to
about their lies.
The one who CAN treat you right.
But you love the pain.
I'm just a mate,
your best friend,
a lover who listens
but you want nothing else.
You only love pain.

For the Friend Zoned

For the people in the friend zone,
I'm sorry they don't appreciate you.
I'm sorry you're stuck on your own,
in love with someone who'll never accept you.
I'm sorry that they don't want you,
they want the idea of you, just not you.
They want the best looking,
with a heart like yours.
But that's rare, so they'll settle
For the candy coated piece of shit.

Infinite Bliss

I see myself in your eyes,
the reflection of me in love.
I feel your love in the skies,
in the light, even at night,
in the moon's radiance
that shines down on us.

Your velvet like lips,
smooth,
dreaming of the day
I get to taste your kiss.

Your love on my lips.
Your love in my arms,
My infinite bliss.

If I believed in monarchy,
Only you would be my queen.

Oh, ruler of my heart,
tell me honestly,
am I truly living in reality?
Is this a dream?
Do you truly love me?

Your Moon

If you were the sun,
I will be your moon.
You will always
find my love
chasing you.

Printed Love

The feeling of your touch,
printed into my fingertips.
A permanent reminder
of our growing love
That could have been bliss,
but now remains
as manifested regret.

One of a Kind

My heart tells no lie.
You are the truth
devouring my mind.

You are the orchid
blooming in a different time.
You are the diamond
found on the surface,
one of a kind.

You are a cloud
travelling the skies.

Loving without sound,
realities you defy.

You are a treasure
that pirates couldn't find.

Nothing Left

You were my weakness
and my strength.
Now that you've left,
what do I have left?

Just the memories
of our dancing sequence.
Just the fading taste of
your kiss's sweetness.

I am an empty shell
without your love.

In all directions

Life

travels

in

all

directions

like

the

words

that

flow

from

my heart.

Know your worth

You want to be loved,
you're scared of being hurt.
You don't know
what you deserve,
because you've always
fallen in the trap of lust.
You're worth more
than what he makes you believe,
don't be deceived.
Your love isn't a commodity,
for guys to defeat.
You deserve more.

Majesty

I see heavens
reflecting in your eyes.
Are you the answer
to the prayers
for which I cried?
You grace the skies,
winds caressing your wings
as you soar and fly.
the majesty of a panther,
a sight defying
the realities of sight.

Life & Love

In all my life,
I've loved and lived.
I failed both times.
I lost what's mine
and didn't appreciate
this gift.

This life.

Let my heart speak

If I were to
let my heart speak,
the words would
be crimson
as its mouth bleeds.
It would complain
that it found no peace,
Of its fluctuation in its beats.
That it fell in love.
That it wasn't enough.
It curses me
for losing her touch.

The Cycle

nothing

lust

love

loving

loved

nothing.

Fleeting Affections

Maybe it was because I loved you too much
that you too ran away with the dust.

Now I remain forever bereft of your touch,
still for a brief moment,
I got to know the magic of heavenly love.

Life is fleeting like your affections,
It is only myself I see now in reflections.

When once upon a time ago,
I would envision both our silhouettes
cast upon the mirror's detection

From strangers to friends,
from friends to lovers,
to strangers again.

The most painful
infinite cycle
Of life to
never end.

The Void

It seems only solitude
shall be my companion.
And If I'm honest too
it will never fill the void
of my heart's canyon.

A life bereft of your love
is certainly not a life to live.
A day without your touch,
A day without your kiss,
is painful enough,
but how am I to
endure all of this?

Heartbreak routine

From nothing
to everything
to nothing again.
From strangers,
to friends,
to lovers,
to strangers again.

This is the routine
of heartbreak.
A cycle that causes
our stars to fade.

The Strength of Women

Your tears aren't a sign of weakness.
It's a sign that you've endured so much
that now your eyes are feeling it.
Your heart is bleeding,
your eyes are leaking,
yet you're still holding it together.
And though,
you don't need to be tough,
you choose to be.

You're amazing.

Writer's Block

Writers block is
when the soul is asleep,

and the heart
is trying to avoid
it's dreams.

My Story, Your Ending

Though it was my story and
I had poured my soul inside it,
you ended the final chapter,
when I suddenly stopped writing.
Stamped by our tears,
we parted whilst crying,
knowing in 10 years,
we will regret that for our love,
we had stopped fighting.

Another Poem

But in the end,
you're just another poem
on the page,
a story in my book
and another memory to fade

Continuous Lies

I continued to love
while you continued to lie,
you continued to live
while I continued to die.

Conversations with the moon

I used to talk
to the moon
about you
every single day,
now the moon

questions me
asking me what
the fuck has changed.
I have no answer,
I don't know what to say.
But the moon realises
the depths of my pain
and no longer asks.

Learning to Love

I wanted to learn
how to live life
and how to love.
It was only in
loving you
that I lived.

My Dream

You are
the dream
for which
I force
myself
to sleep
to see.

Blinded Love

You've doomed an innocent soul,
she's going to suffer in this life.
How could you possibly be so cold,
She was so innocent with
nothing but love in her eyes.

She was ready to give you her world,
but you had something else in mind.
You destroyed her with but a few words
And now she understands why
they say love is blind.

Her Wilting Heart

Beyond those screaming droplets
and bleeding tears,
beyond that mind that was honest
is a heart filled with fear.
Beyond a shattered will
beyond the shadow's hill . . .

Her heart is wilting away,
Corroding;
subject to decay.

And you are the reason
for all of this.

What makes you smile

If it makes you smile,
I will bring all of the star's down.
Just for the moment
in which I can hear
your heart's sound.

Heart's Subjugation

When we find
hearts subjugated,
It is enslaved
by love.

By affections,
It is suffocated,
yet we consume it
until we are
drunk.

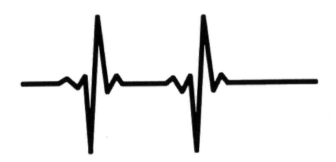

Your Shadow

Your shadow is
still here
but it's just
an empty touch
that can't catch
any of my
tears.

You're not her

I loved who
I thought you were.
The love
yet lives
even though
you're not her.

Dissect my heart

Dissect my heart and find
your name pumps through
each blood vessel
until the day I die.

My love for you
is like a poison
running through my veins.
Yet strange,
life seems frozen
and this gives me
more joy than pain.

Entrancing Beauty

Your beauty is entrancing, hypnotising
like the visions of a self-induced fantasy.
You've made more than a difference to my life,
you've enhanced it,

and you certainly mean more to me than
most of my friends and family.
Your beauty is the kind one
can't stop oneself from glancing,

confident people making moves and
advancing,
like a diamond that causes star struck
gazes,
projected desires are chanted.

I used to converse with the moon,
its radiance trapped me, never did I think a
truer beauty existed till your words had
grasped me.

The stars are dim in comparison to your awe,
though constellations in congregations are
expanding,
you are nothing like anything ever seen
before.

You are the gravitational centre of this
universe,
a grace so commanding,
It seems my dreams are relapsing,
or are the angels really at war?

Fighting in their envy, jealous of your base
purity,
your heart of poetry,
complaining of their own obscurity,
the heavens will be emptied.
You have the power to bless lives
with a simple glance or word,
your sentences are serenades
that paint the life of the world.

A single sentence you speak
grants healing when reading,
Everything in this world is measurable
except your worth.

You are always kept in my thoughts,
in my prayers,
in the hopes that you are kept safe and
healthy,
and you are granted success in all of your
affairs.

Remember; joy in yourself is success,
your talent means you're wealthy,
may the journey of this life
keep you happy and give you plenty,
a blessing to my life, dear beloved, healer of
all despair.

Silent Nights

It's always on a silent night, alone with my
mind,
alone with my thoughts, a swell in my eyes,
uncontrollable twitches in my sighs.
It's a dark time, there's no light,
I'm at a war trying to decide who's right.
My heart or my mind?

Who's gonna stop me from drowning in my
tears,
who's gonna stop me from being devoured by
my fears?

My broken heart still wishes she was here,
nothing else has ever been so clear.

But the pain continues to spread over the
years,
like a drop of poison in the sound of my
prayers.

I'm screaming to be heard,
but the willingly deaf will never hear my
words.
There is a dark veil shadowing the world.
Ignorance.

The devil on my shoulder, like an eagle
perched,
there is no water that could ever quench my
thirst.
My inspiration runs dry as my soul loses it's
worth.
God, it hurts.

Cursing the day of my birth,

with every breath that passes,
it seems I myself am cursed.

I will never be able to tame this pain,
it's loose, wild and spontaneous like a Carolina
flame.
Nothing shall extinguish its heat,
not the mightiest of downpours or infinite
rains,
not the end of days, not the sun's eclipse,
not even if the entire ocean was poured upon
its place.

This pain shall never end.
There is no healing for a heart
that will never mend.
I mean I could pretend,
a fake smile will fool everyone
except myself.

A Night shift sonnet

6AM dawns, clouds like
white candy floss,
Floating across the skies
like they were lost.

A hiding sun, disguised,
amongst the horizon's plot.
Waiting for its time to rise,
and awaken the world
to a day that's too hot.

As I travel home from
my working night,
I see trees standing tall
with pride and might.

The breeze tickling leaves,
a whispering caress
so simple and light.

Cars driving straight in line,
as they pass by,
ruling the roads with their tyres.

My tired eyes are
recording this image
To be forgotten till the next night.

Birds taking flight,
powerful wings
that cleave the skies,
whilst in melodies they sing,
flapping away as they fly.

Dying thoughts in my mind
fading away as brain pleas for sleep.
This journey takes some time,
so, I find myself lost in day dreams.

visualising desires wished by me,
yet hope is just a feeling of need.
I refuse to open my heart,
in fear of letting flow my eyes.

Streaming tears cascading
as my emotions depart
and memories fill my head again,
Ones I despise.

I hate that this pain remains,
lingering like my mental health.

It makes me want to
take my showers in the rain
and drown in the sorrow of myself.

The day reminds me of too much,
there's too much time
to reminisce of her touch, of her love,
the one that's broken my life.

Can I stop thinking of us?
If Romeo was thought to have
loved Juliet,
then what will my love's legacy tell
Future generations of us? Of what was?

And Let the Sun Rise Again

Contact Info:

Maavi Raja

Twitter: @MaaviPoet
Instagram: @MaaviPoet

Email: maavipoet@gmail.com

22270272R00066

Printed in Great Britain
by Amazon